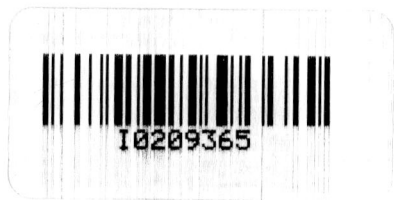

Buffalo Brewers Association

Brewers Convention 1897 in Buffalo, NY

Buffalo Brewers Association

Brewers Convention 1897 in Buffalo, NY

ISBN/EAN: 9783742803603

Manufactured in Europe, USA, Canada, Australia, Japa

Cover: Foto ©Gila Hanssen / pixelio.de

Manufactured and distributed by brebook publishing software (www.brebook.com)

Buffalo Brewers Association

Brewers Convention 1897 in Buffalo, NY

Buffalo
Brewers'
Association,

SOUVENIR OF

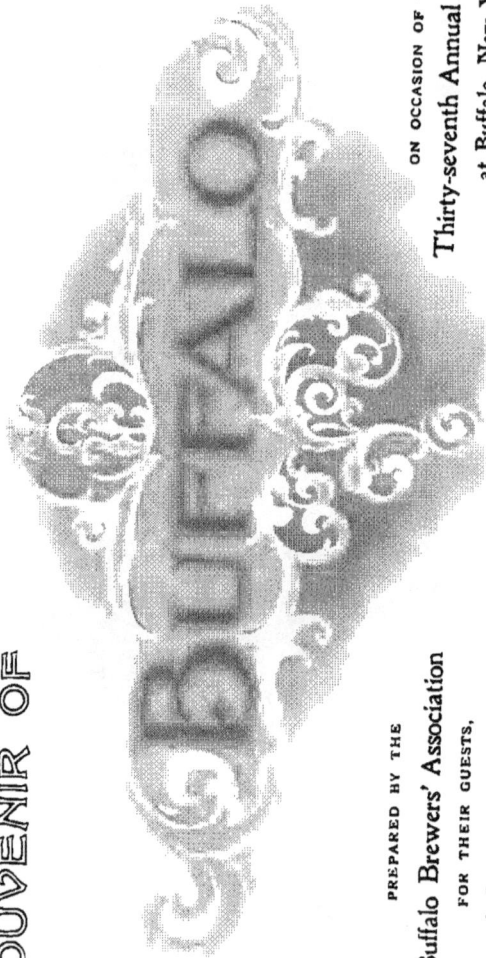

BUFFALO

PREPARED BY THE

Buffalo Brewers' Association

FOR THEIR GUESTS,

The United States Brewers' Association,

ON OCCASION OF THE

Thirty-seventh Annual Convention

at Buffalo, New York,

June, 1897.

MADE IN

THE COMPLETE ART-PRINTING WORKS
OF
THE MATTHEWS-NORTHRUP CO.
BUFFALO, N. Y.
18680

GREETING. Buffalo, long known as the "Queen City of the Lakes," and because of recent development now inaptly named the "Electric City," is proud to be honored by the visit of such a reputable representative body as the United States Brewers' Association, which comes within her borders to hold its thirty-seventh annual convention. She is also proud to believe that she has within those borders attractions and advantages which will commend themselves to the favorable attention of her guests and conduce greatly to their enjoyment. May they hear the echoes of a hearty welcome-greeting wafted on the gentle breezes that sweep softly over the waters of Lake Erie, or hear them murmuring among the foliage of our many tree-bordered avenues. May those echoes be heard resounding o'er the verdure of our parks, among the ripplings of the mighty river flowing so grandly onward from lake to lake, in the assembly halls and wherever the business or pleasure of her guests may lead them.

Should the elements prove gracious, her guests will find delight in her pleasant climate and in her pure and healthful atmosphere. They will admire her

well-paved streets, the fine landscape of her park system and the manifold attractions of her lake and river frontage. They will behold on every hand evidences of thrift and enterprise; they will see a great city emerging from the chrysalis condition of provincialism into the full glory of municipal vigor and progressiveness. About her harbor and along the steel highways which extend east, west, north and south, they will note those signs which proclaim her as the chief gateway to the traffic of the great lakes, to the vast lumber forests and wide-spread grain fields of the northwest and the coal mines of the east and south. They will witness the latest and greatest manifestation of the wonders of applied science in the constant use of electric power generated by the harnessed current of the Niagara and transmitted hither from the famous cataract to the great street railway system. They will see much more that will tend to enhance the claims of Buffalo to recognition as a great and growing city, but above and beyond all these material things will be the genial smiles and hearty hand-shakes that will greet the visitors and make them believe that the cries of "Welcome!" and "Willkommen!" which will resound on every hand, mean something more than noisy words.

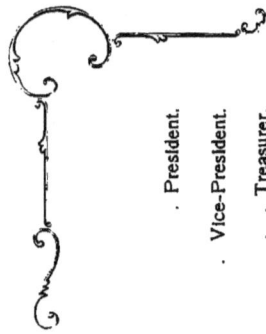

Officers.

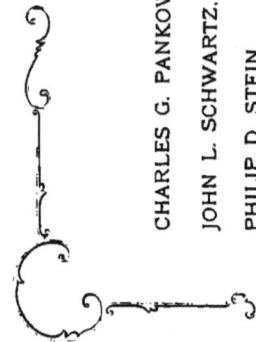

CHARLES G. PANKOW.	. President.
JOHN L. SCHWARTZ,	. Vice-President.
PHILIP D. STEIN,	. . Treasurer.
JACOB F. KUHN, . . .	. Secretary.
CHRISTIAN TRAPP. .	. Ass't Secretary.

Committees.

Finance and Executive Committee.

E. G. S. MILLER,   PHILIP D. STEIN,   GEORGE C. GINTHER,
    PHILIP G. SCHAEFER,   WILLIAM SIMON,
JOHN KREITNER,   JOHN L. SCHWARTZ.

Entertainment Committee.

WM. T. BECKER,   GEORGE DITTLY,   JULIUS SCHEU,
    JOHN HONECKER,   OSCAR P. ROCHEVOT,
WILLIAM F. DUCKWITZ,   JOHN WEYAND.

Committee on Badges.

PHILIP D. STEIN,   EUGENE IRR,   JULIUS BINZ.

Reception Committee:

ROBERT F. SCHELLING,   SIMON MERGENHAGEN,   JOS. P. SCHATTNER,
GEORGE F. LUTZ,   P. REINLAENDER,   C. HAMMER,   JOHN A. MILLER,
    JACOB G. LANG,   GEORGE SANDROCK,   WM. J. VOELKER,
JOS. G. SCHAFF,   JOSEPH PHILLIPS,   CHARLES WEYAND,

Hotel and Railroad Committee.

PHILIP G. SCHAEFER,   GEORGE DITTLY,   FRANK J. ILLIG,
    JOHN KREITNER,   GEORGE C. GINTHER.

Souvenir Committee.

GEORGE C. GINTHER,   WM. F. DUCKWITZ,   OSCAR P. ROCHEVOT,
    JOHN L. SCHWARTZ.

Banquet Committee.

CHARLES G. PANKOW,   PHILIP G. SCHAEFER,   E. G. S. MILLER,
    GEORGE C. GINTHER,   WM. T. BECKER,
JOHN L. SCHWARTZ,   FRANK J. ILLIG,   JOHN KREITNER.

LOUIS FREUND,   JOHN C. SCHENK,
    L. BURGWEGER,   WM. MILLER,
GEO. A. LEWIS.

Members.

List of Members.	Representatives.	Alternates.
MAGNUS BECK BREWING CO.,	GEO. C. GINTHER,	ROBERT F. SCHELLING.
THE BUFFALO CO-OPERATIVE BREWING CO.,	JOHN HONECKER,	SIMON MERGENHAGEN.
THE BROADWAY BREWING CO.,	CHARLES BELZER,	JOS. P. SCHATTNER.
THE CLINTON CO-OPERATIVE BREWING CO.,	CHAS. G. PANKOW,	LOUIS FREUND.
THE EAST BUFFALO BREWING CO.,	WM. T. BECKER,	JOHN C. SCHENK.
GERMAN AMERICAN BREWING CO.,	GEORGE DITTLY,	GEORGE F. LUTZ.
GAMBRINUS BREWING CO.,	EUGENE IRR,	P. REINLAENDER.
GERMANIA BREWING CO.,	FRANK J. ILLIG,	C. HAMMER.
THE INTERNATIONAL BREWING CO.,	JULIUS SCHEU,	JOHN A. MILLER.
IROQUOIS BREWING CO.,	JOHN KREITNER,	L. BURGWEGER.
THE KALTENBACH BREWING CO.,	PHILIP D. STEIN,	WM. MILLER.
THE GERHARD LANG BREWERY,	EDWIN G. S. MILLER,	JACOB G. LANG.
LAKE VIEW BREWING CO.,	PHILIP G. SCHAEFER,	GEORGE SANDROCK.
THE LION BREWERY,	OSCAR P. ROCHEVOT,	WM. J. VOELKER.
THE J. SCHUESLER BREWING CO.,	WILLIAM SIMON,	JOS. G. SCHAFF.
THE STAR BREWERY,	JOHN L. SCHWARTZ,	JOSEPH PHILLIPS.
CHRISTIAN WEYAND BREWING CO.,	JOHN A. WEYAND,	CHARLES WEYAND.
ZIEGELE BREWING CO.,	WM. F. DUCKWITZ.	GEO. A. LEWIS.

ADOLF KUHN.

MAGNUS BECK.

GERHARD LANG.

F. JÖST

THE BREWING INDUSTRY.

HIS BRANCH of industrial enterprise furnishes one of the important items in the large aggregate of the trade of Buffalo, and has for many years largely contributed to the wonderful prosperity and growth of the city. Not only in the aggregate of its output, but in the quality of the product as well, Buffalo is a successful rival of any city of the Union, both in the home and export trade. The business was inaugurated synchronously with the incorporation of Buffalo as a city, and with its wonderful growth in all that constitutes material prosperity the brewing business — malting, bottling, and kindred interests — have kept even pace.

It is ascertained from the best information obtainable, that previous to 1840 there were in this city five (5) breweries, with a capacity of from one to nine (9) barrel kettles each.

The pioneer in this important enterprise was Jacob Roos, whose plant was located in what was then called "Sandy Town"— between Church and York streets, and beyond the Erie Canal, near the Old Stone House. Early in the forties he purchased the land lying between Hickory and Pratt streets, below Batavia Street, now Broadway, where the present fine buildings of the Iroquois Brewing Co. are situated, the present plant having a capacity of 90,000 barrels annually.

In 1840 Messrs. J. F. Schanzlin & Hoffman established a brewery at the corner of Main and St. Paul streets — a stone building and brew house were located here. Part of the stone building

was used as a restaurant ; these buildings are to-day the same as in 1840, and are now used as tenements. In 1842 the firm was dissolved, Mr. Hoffman continuing the business, and Mr. Schanzlin purchased a number of acres of ground on the corner of Main Street, Delavan Avenue, and Scajaquada Creek, and now known as the Buffalo Athletic Field. He erected here a large brew house and a fine dwelling and restaurant, which was patronized by many of the most prominent citizens of Buffalo in those days. The brew house was torn down but the dwelling house, restaurant and barn remain, and are occupied as tenements.

The third brewery established in this city was that of Joseph Friedman, on Oak Street near Tupper, where St. Marcus Church now stands. He erected here a brew house, dwelling and restaurant, and while beer was sold in the saloons at that time for 5 cents per quart, he sold his product at six pence or 6¼ cents per quart, from which fact he was called "sixpencer," which so advertised him that he did a lucrative business. The plant in later years passed into the hands of Beck & Baumgartner, and it was here that Magnus Beck laid the foundation of the present Magnus Beck Brewing Co.'s extensive business, which is now conducted on both corners of North Division and Spring streets, with a capacity of 200,000 barrels per annum. Mr. Baumgartner erected his brewery corner of Exchange and Van Rensselaer streets, but he died soon afterwards.

The next in order of time was the establishment of Phil. Born, corner of Genesee and Jefferson streets. This brewery was the most modern of its day. Mr. Born died in 1848, and the business was conducted by his widow and Jacob Weppner, under the old firm name. In 1862 Gerhard Lang was married to the oldest daughter of Mr Born and took the place of Mr. Weppner, the firm becoming Born & Lang, and it was here that the latter began his career, which brought him great wealth and prominence in this field of industrial enterprise.

Mr. Lang purchased the Cobb Farm, corner of Best and Jefferson streets, where at present the imposing buildings and extensive plant of the Gerhard Lang Park Brewery is located, with a capacity of 200,000 barrels annually.

Godfrey Heiser was the next to engage in the business, and carried on his trade on Seneca Street below Chicago Street. In 1864 the business passed into the hands of Godfrey Heiser, Jr., and Jacob Holzer, both of whom died within a few years, and the business was discontinued.

In 1863 there were 35 breweries in successful operation in this city, conducted by the following well-known brewers: Albert Ziegele, corner of Main and Virginia streets; Born & Lang, corner of Genesee and Jefferson streets; Magnus Beck, corner of North Division and Spring streets; Jacob Scheu, corner of Genesee and Spring streets; J. F. Schanzlin, corner of Main Street and Delevan Avenue; Charles Gerber, corner of Main Street and Burton Alley; Mushall & Appert, Main Street near Goodell Street; John Schuesler, corner of Emslie and Clinton streets; George Roos, Roos Street; F. X. Kaltenbach, Lutheran Street; Fritz Albrecht, 815 Broadway; George Weber, 652 Broadway; Nicholas Hiemenz, Broadway, opposite St. Mary's Church; Fritz Loersch, Genesee Street, near Hickory Street; David Haas, southwest corner of Cherry and Spring streets; George Rochevot, southeast corner of Cherry and Spring streets; Christ Becker, corner of Genesee and Jefferson streets; Franz Welde, Main Street, opposite Summer Street; Joseph L. Haberstro, corner of Main and High streets; Michael Hoelner, corner of High and Michigan streets; Jacob Baumgartner, corner of Exchange and Van Rensselaer streets; Fritz Lang, corner of Genesee and Grey streets; Gottlieb Bodemer, Genesee Street, near Walden Avenue; Chris Loos, 18 West Bennett Street; Heiser & Holzer, Seneca Street, below Chicago Street; F. J. Jost, corner of Broadway and Pratt Street; Gareis & Knobloch, Oak near Tupper Street; Baldus & Schleucher, corner of Clinton and Cedar streets; John G. Roehrer, corner of Jefferson and Best streets; William Moffatt, ale brewery, Morgan Street; Hugh Boyle, ale brewery, St. Paul Street; Wm. W. Sloan, corner of Exchange and Van Rensselaer streets.

While the manufacture of beer in the year 1863 was 152,000 barrels, in 1896 the product of the Buffalo breweries aggregated 652,340 barrels, while the number of breweries decreased from 35 in 1863 to 19 in 1896, an illustration not only of the survival of the fittest, but of their steady growth and success.

In 1872, when the price of raw materials was very high, and the breweries were doing business at a loss, an organization of the brewers of Buffalo was effected to fix the price of their product and to protect themselves from loss.

The first regular meeting was held on the second Tuesday of January, 1873, over Donald Bain's Brewers' Supply store, at No. 557 Main Street, and the following were elected officers of the organization: President, Gerhard Lang; Vice-President, Magnus Beck; Treasurer, F. J. Jost; Secretary, Jacob F. Kuhn.

A resolution was adopted at this meeting to admit maltsters, hop dealers, and kindred trades, as associate members.

At the regular meeting in January, 1875, Mr. Jacob Scheu was elected vice-president in place of Magnus Beck, resigned.

In January, 1878, the following were elected officers: President, Albert Ziegele; Vice-President, Joseph L. Haberstro; Treasurer, John Schuesler; Secretary, Jacob F. Kuhn.

During the first week in June, 1880, the United States Brewers' Convention was held in this city, and the occasion was one of great interest and pleasure, and the event will long be remembered as one of importance and benefit to this branch of industry.

From January 1, 1882, to January 1, 1886, the organization had only a nominal existence. A re-organization, however, was effected in May, 1887, and officers were elected as follows: President, Joseph Timmerman; Vice-President, August Beck; Treasurer, George Rochevot; Secretary, Jacob F. Kuhn. A new constitution and by-laws were adopted.

At the meeting in May, 1890, Charles G. Pankow was elected President; John A. Weyand, Vice-President; the Secretary and Treasurer being re-elected. Mr. Rochevot resigned his office as treasurer in 1891, and Julius Binz was elected to fill the vacancy. In September, 1893, the following were elected to fill the offices, as follows: President, Charles G. Pankow; Vice-President, J. W. Niederpruem; and the Secretary and Treasurer were re-elected. Mr. Binz resigned his position as treasurer December, 1894, and Edwin G. S. Miller was elected in his stead: Mr. Miller resigned December, 1896. The officers are at present as follows: President, Charles G. Pankow; Vice-President, John L. Schwartz; Treasurer, Phillp D. Stein; Secretary, J. F. Kuhn.

At present there are 19 breweries in successful operation, and located as follows: The Magnus Beck Brewing Co., on both corners of North Division and Spring streets; The Buffalo Co-Operative Brewing Co., corner of High and Michigan streets; The Broadway Brewing Co., 15 Broadway; The Clinton Co-Operative Brewing Co., 10-24 West Bennett Street; The East Buffalo Brewing Co., 300 Emslie Street; The German-American Brewing Co., 11 High Street; The Gambrinus Brewery Co., 652 Broadway; The Germania Brewing Co., 1615 Broadway; The International Brewing Co., 1078 Niagara Street; The Iroquois Brewing Co., 230 Pratt Street; The Kaltenbach Brewing Co., Pratt Street, between Eagle and Clinton streets; The Gerhard Lang Brewery, corner of Best and Jefferson streets; The Lake View Brewing Co. 132 Lake View Avenue; The Lion Brewery, 1037 Jefferson Street; The J. Schuesler Brewing Co. 143 Emslie Street; The Star Brewery, corner of Spring and Cherry streets; The C. Weyand Brewing Co., 785 Main Street; The Ziegele Brewing Co., corner of Washington and Virginia streets; Henry C. Moffatt, ale brewer, corner Morgan and Mohawk streets.

Magnus Beck Brewing Co.

MAGNUS BECK, the founder of the immense brewing plant situated on the north and south sides of North Division and Spring streets, was born in the year 1819 at Osterhoffen, Wurttemberg, Germany, and died in Buffalo, May 29, 1883, mourned as a kind and loving father, and a tried and true, generous and liberal-minded friend and benefactor. Two sons, Edward and Frank M., and one daughter, Mrs. Adam J. Benzing, survive him. When but 17 years old Mr. Beck was apprenticed to a brewer in Wurtzog, Wurttemberg, Germany. After his apprenticeship he went to Ulm, Wurttemberg, and later to Frauenenburg.

In 1850, Mr. Beck came direct to Buffalo, and was for two years the valued foreman of the Godfrey Heiser's brewery on Seneca Street. At this time he accepted the position as brewmaster for the Kaltenbach Brewery, in which position he gave eminently satisfactory service; but Dame Fortune had laid other plans for his activity, and in 1855 he formed the partnership of Beck & Baumgartner, with a brewing plant on Oak, near Tupper Street. This partnership was dissolved in 1860. Under the sole energy and ability of Mr. Beck the business grew to such proportions that in 1865 the present site was purchased, upon which buildings were erected and equipped with what was then the most modern and best machinery used in brewing practice. This policy of advancement has been strictly followed by his successors, who have kept in touch with the rapid increase in the volume of business transacted each year, in the way of adoption of new methods, and the substitution of new machinery for old, until, at the present time, the plant is the most complete and extensive of its kind, and its product excelled by none.

In 1873 the death of Mrs. Beck inflicted the greatest sorrow of his life. She was Miss Flora Hertzog, whom he first met in Frauenenter, Switzerland, and who followed him to the New World in 1851. In the same year they were married, and in the many years of married life which followed she contributed not a little to the success of her worthy husband.

After the death of Mr. Beck, in 1883, his estate carried on the business until the formation of the stock company in 1886. The capacity of the plant, at the time, was 35,000 barrels yearly. The last ten years have brought many gratifying results to the company. To-day it is one of the largest breweries in Buffalo, with an annual capacity of over 200,000 barrels, which speaks volumes for the product, the wisdom, sagacity and marked ability of the executive officers of the company, at the head of which is Mr. William J. Conners, President; Frank Beck, Vice-President; John T. Clarls, Secretary; Robert F. Schelling, Treasurer; and George C. Ginther, Manager.

The Buffalo Co-Operative Brewing Co.

FEBRUARY 20, 1880, one of the most successful breweries ever started in Buffalo first drew its official breath, namely. The Buffalo Co-Operative Brewing Co., situated on the corner of High and Michigan streets, of which Jacob Manhardt was elected president; P. Mergenhagen, vice-president; O. Banghard, secretary, and C. Schuler, treasurer, with a Board of Auditors composed of F. Rieck, J. Honecker, and Henry George, with Louis Eydl as Superintendent. The object of the company was merely to supply the individual wants of its members; It being compulsory for all stockholders to be dealers, no limit being placed on their requirements. The capacity of the plant at this time was 10,000 barrels per year, which did not nearly meet the demand. The beverage manufactured was of such high grade, and met with such general favor among consumers, the demand being so great, that it was finally deemed wise to call a meeting of the stockholders to discuss the advisability of changing the articles so as to make it possible to sell direct to any dealer or consumer, whether holding stock in the company or not. Receiving unanimous approval, the by-laws were changed accordingly.

Shortly after, the ice house caved in, inflicting a serious loss, but arrangements were soon made and operations were continued, until, five years later, the company was re-incorporated by a special act, the most striking article being that no stockholder should have more than one vote in deciding questions pertaining to its affairs, irrespective of the number of shares held, thus giving the holder of a few shares equal right with holders of many shares, a commendable principle based on the broad lines of equity and justice, furnishing an almost unparalleled example of united and harmonious action among members of a company banded together for mutual financial welfare and support. In June, 1887, progress was checked by a disastrous fire, causing a financial loss of $30,000. The damage was so great that the old site was cleaned up and new buildings erected and equipped with the most modern machinery for brewing, the capacity being 100,000 barrels per annum.

The present executive officers are John Honecker, president; Aug. Kempff, vice-president; C. R. Rauch, treasurer; and S. Mergenhagen, secretary, with the following board of directors: Alex. Selle, J. Schroder, S. Mergenhagen, J. Beierlein, B. Weber and William Kessler. How well and efficiently the interests of the company have been looked after can best be illustrated by the gratifying increase in the volume of business transacted. Within a period of ten years, buildings have been erected, machinery purchased and installed regardless of cost, with an annual output of over 41,000 barrels, so that the management, by its vigorous and progressive policy, has earned the approbation and gratitude of the stockholders.

The Broadway Brewing and Malting Company.

THE BROADWAY is located the Broadway Brewing and Malting Company, one of Buffalo's prominent breweries. It enjoys the distinction of being one of the oldest and most successful. From a modest beginning in 1852, it passed through different stages of prosperity, until, in 1880, Julius Binz, became proprietor. In 1884, Mr. Binz added the malting business to his concern, and this is now the principal feature. In 1886, the plant was entirely rebuilt, and machinery of the newest and best kind installed at an enormous expense.

In 1887, a stock company was formed, with a capitalization of $100,000, and the premises occupied comprise the entire block bounded by Broadway, Shumway and Smith streets. Since the organization of the stock company the increase of business has been most gratifying to the stockholders and the executive officers, and the products of the company are shipped daily to many large cities of the Union. The malting department is a private enterprise, belonging solely to Mr. Binz, and in no way is it connected with the company. Mr. Binz has one of the finest malt houses in the city, and the annual output is from two to three hundred thousand bushels. The quality of the beer manufactured by the Broadway Brewery is of the highest grade, and all of the machinery used in its production is of the latest type, and have an aggregate capacity of 100 tons. The necessary power for the operation and lighting of this plant is furnished by natural gas, which was discovered on the premises of the company in 1890. The buildings are constructed of brick, stone and iron, and are absolutely fire-proof.

The present officers of the company are : Julius Binz, president, Peter Vogt, vice-president, and Joseph Schattner, secretary. With Julius and Charles W. Belzer they also comprise the Board of Directors.

Mr. Julius Binz, the chief executive officer, was born in Germany in 1847, and was but twenty years old when he arrived in Buffalo, since which time his inherent successful qualities have enabled him to rapidly come to the front in all of his undertakings. Mr. Binz ranks to-day as one of the wealthiest brewers in the country, and while he has large interests outside of the malting and brewing business, he gives most of his attention to the latter. He enjoys an enviable reputation as a maltster, and is conceded to be one of the best authorities on raw material.

The Hon. Mathias Rohr, one of Buffalo's prominent Germans, was the president of the company for some time previous to the election of Mr. Binz.

The Clinton Co-Operative Brewing Co.

ROBABLY no more ably managed brewery exists in the United States than the Clinton Co-operative Brewing Company. It was established in 1881, with a capital of $100,000. The stock is now over 100 per centum above par, and 10 per cent. dividends have been paid every year to the stockholders since 1886. Of course, the quality of the beer, brewed by one of the most expert brewmasters In the country, has had much to do with the growth of the business. From an annual output of 6,000 barrels for the year ending June 1, 1882, it has increased from year to year, and now reaches about 20,000 barrels. The premises are situated at Nos. 10 to 24 West Bennett Street, between Clinton and William, opposite the Clinton Market. A great deal of money has been expended by the present company In remodeling the buildings and equipping them with the most modern machinery and Improvements, making its capacity 40,000 barrels per annum. The plant is built of brick and stone, the latest addition being a three-story brick building, containing a bottling works, with the latest improvements. Only the best hops and malt that money can buy are used, and no expense or effort is spared in making the product unexcelled. The different brands of beer manufactured are well liked, and are sold principally in Buffalo, with Eastern Pennsylvania and Western New York connections. Frequent analysis of the beer has fully established its purity.

The executive officers are : Charles G. Pankow, president, Frederick H. Yuhl, vice-president, Louis Freund, treasurer, and Louis Baltz, secretary.

Mr. Charles G. Pankow was born in Germany in 1851, and came to Buffalo in 1864. He was elected president in 1882, and with the exception of one year, has held this office ever since. Mr. Pankow is also the esteemed president of the Buffalo Brewers Association, and as a Commissioner of Public Works for the city of Buffalo has an enviable record.

Mr. Frederick Yuhl was born in Buffalo in 1849. He became a stockholder in 1881, and was elected vice-president in 1891.

Mr. Louis Freund was born in Alsace in 1835, and in 1881 became a stockholder. He has held his present position from the date of the incorporation of the company. Mr. Freund is an experienced business man of undoubted integrity. He has broad and progressive ideas, and is eminently fitted for the position he holds.

Mr. Louis Baltz, the secretary, was born in Germany in 1846. He was elected to his present position in 1885.

The East Buffalo Brewing Company.

ARLY in the spring of 1887 The East Buffalo Brewing Company was incorporated, and assumed control August 1, 1887, of the John M. Luippold Brewery. On the present site, in 1867, in connection with William Voetsch, Mr. Luippold organized and operated the brewery until its purchase by the present company. A continuous prosperity and increase in sales has brought the firm to its present high standing, and has necessitated the additions of new buildings constructed upon modern ideas from the best of material, of stone, brick and steel.

The plant has a frontage of 210 feet on Emslie Street, running through to Watson 217 feet, the whole of which is built to form a square, with a large court-yard in the center. The brewery buildings, comprising brew house, stock house, racking and wash rooms, with refrigerating plant, have capacity for more than an annual output of 100,000 barrels. The brew house, a fire-proof structure 42 x 52 feet, five stories high, is a model of perfection and simplicity, and will bear inspection by the most critical.

On the ground floor of the three-story engine room, a building 26 x 72 feet, are located the refrigerating machines — a 75-ton De La Vergne and a 30-ton Eclipse — a 50 horse-power engine, six pumps, used for various purposes, and a 600 direct-connected dynamo for electric lights, etc. The upper floors are used for ice jacks, beer and ammonia coolers.

The stock house, 80 x 106 feet, four stories in height, is used exclusively for fermenting, storage and chip cask rooms. This is also a fire-proof building.

The racking and wash rooms adjoin the stock house on the south. The boiler house and pitching buildings connect engine rooms on the north. The bottling works and barns face Watson Street on the west.

The firm brews but one kind of beer, their old stock lager, the quality of which is surpassed by none.

The present management consists of the following gentlemen: Henry W. Brendel, president: Wm. T. Becker, vice-president: John C. Schenk, secretary and manager: and George Wesp, treasurer.

German-American Brewing Co.

THE GERMAN-AMERICAN BREWING CO. has a large and beautiful brewery located corner Main and High streets. This company was organized September 1, 1885, and purchased the old and established business of Jos. L. Haberstro. The output of the brewery at the time the company took possession was less than 20,000 barrels yearly, which has since been increased to over 75,000 barrels, the sales amounting to 35,000 barrels, an increase of 27,000,— the previous sales being 8,000 barrels annually,— a fact speaking well for the management and the general favor with which its pure and wholesome product has been received by the public.

In 1893 a new brew house was erected. Although continual improvements had been made to the old plant, the new building was found a necessity to meet the demands, and the stockholders decided to erect one, which was completed in 1894. It is built upon the site of the old plant and cost upwards of $125,000. In the erection of this new building special care was taken by the management and architect to make it one of the most complete plants in this section of the country, and an inspection of the plant will convince anybody that they have succeeded in their efforts. Located, as it is, at the highest point in the city, this, together with the architectural beauty of the buildings, the modern machinery and completeness of the inside arrangements, makes it an ideal brewery in every respect.

In 1896, the new building at the corner of Main and High streets was completed, at a cost of about $75,000, which is very complete and modern. It contains a first-class restaurant and roof garden, under the able management of W. H. Jaeger; also, a large and beautiful concert hall, as well as the club rooms of the Buffalo Orpheus Singing Society. Special effort was made by the architect in its erection to fully arrange for the convenience of the public, and evidences of his success in this direction can be noticed on all sides.

The directors of the company in 1885 were Geo. Dittly, Wm. Henrich, Geo. F. Lutz, John F. Barth, Mathias Storck, Ernst Bamberg, L. Hauenstein, Ignatz Schiesel and Jacob Stauch.

Mr. Dittly was elected the first president and general manager, which position he has since filled, and much of the success of the company is directly due to his zeal, ability and untiring efforts in its behalf.

The present board of directors are Geo. Dittly, Geo. F. Lutz, John F. Barth, Mathias Storck, Ernst Bamberg, Ignatz Schiesel, Andrew Lieber, Alois Reger, and F. A. Menge.

N THE latter part of August, 1891, Mr. Eugene Irr — who for twenty years had experience in the beer-brewing business of this city — in company with Conrad Hammer, an expert brewer, Peter Reinlaender, Fred. Mersmann and Conrad Klemm, formed a co-partnership for the purpose of engaging in the brewing of standard lager. After carefully considering the locality and facilities for a first-class plant, it was found that the well-known Union Brewery of Jacob F. Kuhn, located at 642-652 Broadway, could be bought at reasonable figures. It was bought without delay. At the time of the purchase the sales amounted to 4,000 barrels. There was but one small ice machine, the casks and kegs badly worn, the rolling stock in worse condition, and buildings needed repairing. However, in face of all this, the extensive cellars, and principally the large frontage and depth (130 by 242 feet) of the property, was an inducement for investment.

The following officers formed the company: Eugene Irr, general superintendent; Conrad Hammer, manager; Conrad Klemm, treasurer; Fred. Mersmann and Peter Reinlaender, directors. The brewery being called "Gambrinus," after the inventor of lager beer. As soon as the new beer was distributed, every one who had a taste of it praised its excellence in purity and strength; in fact, "Gambrinus Beer" became the talk of the town. With persistent soliciting and patience in finding good customers, Mr. Irr soon raised the sales.

The demand for Gambrinus Lager Beer became general. To supply this, two new boilers had to be bought, a new (50 ton) ice machine, with additional piping throughout cellars, was required, larger fermenting tubs, casks and more kegs; the rolling stock had to be increased, etc., etc.; also, additional buildings erected, all on account of the increase in trade.

About the year 1893 the company added a Beer Bottling Department, which, at this writing, has increased to such an extent that to one delivery wagon, in 1893, the company has added four new covered wagons. Thus, through the untiring energy of the superintendent, Mr. Irr. the sales amounted to 20,000 barrels for the last fiscal year.

But, as space does not allow additional facts to prove the increasing popularity of the Gambrinus Brewing Company's lager, we conclude with naming the officers of the company: Eugene Irr, superintendent and manager; John E. Fitzpatrick, chief engineer. Officers and directors of the board: Fred. Mersmann, president; Peter Reinlaender, vice-president; Eugene Irr, secretary; Geo. Kempf, treasurer; John E. Fitzpatrick, M. Schiesel, Con. Klemm, H. J. Rengel, directors.

Germania Brewing Company.

HEN THE Germania Brewing Company, which has always been regarded as one of the best located in Buffalo, was started by Conrad Hammer in 1893, its capacity was but 15,000 barrels. This has steadily increased until now it is 35,000 barrels, with a splendid chance for advancement under its present shrewd and progressive management. The plant of the company is located at 1615 Broadway, and occupies a space of 41,316 square feet. A new building, size 30 x 50 feet, has just been erected to take care of the bottling trade, which represents an output of 35 barrels per week. The principal buildings are of brick and are absolutely fire-proof. One Case refrigerating machine of 30 tons capacity is used. The driving force is furnished by a 50 horse-power Tifft engine. The quality of the beer manufactured by this company is excelled by none for purity and wholesomeness, and the greatly increase of patrons is the best evidence of its popularity. The utmost care is observed in its manufacture, and neither time nor money is spared in keeping the product up to its present high standard.

In 1894, the business was incorporated with a capitalization of $10,000, which has since been increased to $50,000. Over $30,000 has been spent in purchasing new machinery, remodeling the old buildings and making additions thereto, to accommodate the increased business, while still greater changes are contemplated for the future. Mr. Hammer, who is one of the best brewmasters in the country, and has had over thirty years' experience in the brewing business, has charge of the brew house, and only the very highest grade of raw material will pass his inspection.

The present officers of the company are : Frank J. Illig, president, treasurer and general manager; Conrad Hammer, vice-president and superintendent ; James Smith, secretary.

The company is indeed fortunate in having a man of Mr. Illig's many attainments at its head. Mr. Illig was born in Buffalo in 1853, and is therefore, only nearing his prime. At an early age he successfully managed a business of his own at 541 William Street, and although in the midst of an active business life, Mr. Illig found time to serve his city in some of the most honorable and responsible positions. In 1888, Mayor Becker appointed him Civil Service Commissioner. A year later he was appointed Police Commissioner, and through his official career, perhaps, no officer was more esteemed by his colleagues. Mr. Illig is a man of exceptionally strong force of character, with keen discernment and unvarying sound judgment. A successful future is undoubtedly in store for the Germania Brewing Company.

HIS COMPANY succeeded the Jacob Scheu brewery, and was incorporated in 1884 with a capital stock of $200,000. The brewery is situated on Niagara Street, corner of Albany Street, with a frontage of 250 feet on Niagara Street and 350 feet on Albany Street, adjoining the tracks of the N. Y. C. & H. R. R. R. at rear, from which there is a switch running within the yards of this brewery, and being the only establishment of its kind in Buffalo having these conveniences, makes the facilities for shipping far superior over others. The office is located at 1088 Niagara Street; the bottling department at 1076 Niagara Street. The premises of this company are open to examination at any time. It challenges investigation as to the purity, strength and age of its beer, so jealous is it of its reputation in this respect. In the selection of the material the utmost care is taken, and only the very choicest of malt and hops are used in its output. Amongst the vast number of saloons in Buffalo the beer is as popular among judges of good quality as any in the United States. Two kinds of beer, the Stock Lager and the Münchener Hof-bräu, are manufactured. These are sold principally in Buffalo and a portion of Pennsylvania and Ohio. The malt-house has a capacity of 75,000 bushels. Since the incorporation of this brewery a vast sum has been expended for sundry improvements, making this establishment an ornament to the "Queen City."

Iroquois Brewing Co.

THE HANDSOMEST and best appointed brewery in Buffalo is the one owned by the Iroquois Brewing Co. It is situated on Pratt Street, between Broadway and William Street, and stands on historic ground —for here, in the year 1830, was established the old Roos Brewery, the first lager-beer brewery in Buffalo. In the year 1892 the Roos Brewery was purchased by the Iroquois Brewing Company. The old buildings were torn down and in their place arose a brewing plant which has not its equal, as far as excellence of architecture, completeness of detail, convenience and modernness of appointments and management are concerned. All the latest inventions in brewing appliances have been utilized, which give the Iroquois many advantages. The capacity is 150,000 barrels. This year's (1897) output will reach about 75,000 barrels, which in itself assures the quality of their product.

The officers are : Leonard Burgweger, president ; John Kreltner, vice-president, and Robert F. Schelling, treasurer.

The Excelsior Brewery.

The Excelsior Brewery.

THE EXCELSIOR BREWERY, owned by the Kaltenbach Brewing Co., was founded by the late F. X. Kaltenbach almost 50 years ago. Mr. Kaltenbach commenced business on a very small basis, the output during the first year (1850) amounting to about 200 barrels, but by indefatigable energy and close attention his business increased so that he was able to remove the brewery from the former small site on Lutheran Alley to the present commodious site on Pratt Street, bounded by Clinton, Eagle and Spring streets.

In 1887, The Kaltenbach Brewing Co. was incorporated with a capital stock of $175,000, and the plant purchased from Messrs. F. X. Kaltenbach and William Miller, at that time the junior partner.

The first officers were: B. F. Gentsch, president; Phil. D. Stein, vice-president; Chas. L. Fink, treasurer; William Miller, secretary. Considerable improvements were made.—Ice machines added and storage capacity increased so that at present the brewery can favorably compare with any of the most modern plants in its line. During its ten years' business the company has made it a special point to build up a reputation for its product by manufacturing nothing but a pure article, and the popularity of its beer proves its success.

The present officers are: Phil. D. Stein, president and manager; Aug. Baetzhold, vice-president; Adam Boeckel, secretary and treasurer, and Wm. Miller, John Lipp, F. J. Henry, F. C. Priess, John Coon and F. A. Kraft, directors.

Mr. Stein was appointed manager in 1888 and elected as president in 1891, and has served as such since without interruption. He was born in Buffalo in 1851. Mr. Stein is a genial, warm-hearted and at the same time careful business man, and has made a great many friends, not only amongst his co-stockholders, but also amongst the business men and citizens in general.

August Baetzhold, the vice-president, need not be introduced, as he is one of the best known men, not only in the city of Buffalo, but all over the State. Mr. Baetzhold is the proprietor of the long established wholesale liquor business which is carried on under his name on Michigan Street, near Broadway. Mr. Baetzhold served a number of years as treasurer of the State Liquor Dealers' Association, and there is hardly a city or village in this State where he is not known by one or the other for his ready wit, activity and straightforwardness.

Adam Boeckel, the secretary and treasurer, is the well-known wholesale grocer, but still better known as Alderman Boeckel. He is one of Buffalo's rising men; honored and beloved by all who have dealings with him, either in business or politics.

The Gerhard Lang Brewery.

GERHARD LANG, the founder of the Gerhard Lang Brewery, was born in 1834, at Flersheim, Germany; he came to Buffalo in 1848, and died here in 1892. In 1862, Mr. Lang assumed control of the Born Brewery, at the corner of Genesee and Jefferson streets, the beginning of an exceptionally successful mercantile career, which was prematurely ended.

In 1875, owing to the demand for increased facilities, Mr. Lang purchased the present site of the Gerhard Lang Brewery, and erected thereon suitable buildings, which, however, have since been added to, until to-day the plant occupies the entire block bounded by Jefferson, Best, Berlin and Dodge streets. The plant is as perfect and effective as skill, science and money can produce.

The Gerhard Lang Brewery is the largest in Buffalo, the annual capacity being over 300,000 barrels. All of the malting is done on the premises, and only the very highest grade of selected Canadian barley is used.

Since 1892, the business has been under the successful management of Edwin G. S. Miller, one of Buffalo's brightest intellects in business circles, who, it may be said, lacks nothing in the way of years of valuable experience and proved ability. The active direction of affairs is shared with Mr. Miller by Jacob G. Lang, son of Gerhard Lang.

Jacob G. Lang was graduated from Dr. Wyatt's School of Technical Brewing, of New York City, in 1894, and after an extensive tour of inspection of the most prominent breweries he returned to Buffalo, bringing to the benefit of the business a valuable store of scientific and technical knowledge which has, in no inconsiderable measure, helped to maintain and raise the high standard of excellence so long enjoyed by the product of the Gerhard Lang Brewery. The open straightforward policy of the management, and its popular personnel, are potent factors that have ever gained for this immense concern hosts of friends and patrons.

Lake View Brewing Co.

Lake View Brewing Co.

FROM the fact that its annual output of 7,500 barrels in 1885 has increased to 36,000 barrels is sufficient evidence that the Lake View Brewing Company is getting its share of the volume of business done in Buffalo. Nothing is spared in the way of skilled and scientific effort to make the one brand of beer manufactured by this company the very finest in quality. Only the best material obtainable is used in its manufacture.

The brewery occupies an advantageous position at the intersection of Lake View and Porter avenues, and covers a space of more than three acres of ground. It also is adjacent to that portion of Buffalo's beautiful park system known as "The Front."

There are two Ballentine machines, one of 55 and one of 65 tons capacity, while, since 1885, more than $110,000 has been spent in remodeling the brewery and in other improvements. Progress is the watchword here, and nothing is allowed to be left undone that will in the slightest degree contribute to the success of the company on the basis of a high grade product for a high grade trade.

The Lake View Brewing Company was incorporated December 21, 1885, with a capital of $150,000. The officers of the company are as follows: George Sandrock, president; Henry Schaefer, vice-president; Henry W. Brendel, secretary and treasurer; Philip G. Schaefer, general manager.

In addition to the officers, T. J. Mahoney, John Basher, Henry Ernst and Otto Millow compose the board of directors.

The Lion Brewery.

EORGE ROCHEVOT, the founder of the Lion Brewery, was born at Rhenish, in Bavaria. 1832, and died in Buffalo in January 29. 1897, age 64 years 1 month 9 days. His sons, who survive him, are actively engaged in the management of the affairs of the brewery.

Mr. Rochevot started in the brewing business in 1857. on Spring and Cherry streets, and removed to the present site (993—1041 Jefferson Street) in 1871. Under his able and effective direction the volume of business increased yearly to such an extent that new buildings and machinery were constantly added until to-day the plant is one of the most extensive in Buffalo.

In 1892, an incorporated stock company was formed with a capitalization of $100,000, with Geo. Rochevot as president and manager; Caroline Rochevot, vice-president; Oscar P. Rochevot, secretary.

All of the malt used is made on the premises, only the very best of American and Canadian barley being utilized. The plant has an area of 121,695 square feet, and contains three Case refrigerating machines, with an aggregate capacity of two hundred and fifteen tons, while two Corliss engines, each of 80 horse-power, supply the necessary driving force. The buildings are constructed entirely of brick, stone and iron, and are fitted throughout with a perfect sprinkling system, every precaution being taken to make them as nearly absolutely fire-proof as possible.

The Lion Brewery caters almost entirely to their large local trade, and makes a specially of three different kinds of beer, i. e., "Celebrated Private Stock," "Bohemian" and "Export," their famous bottled lager. designed especially for family and club use. All of these brands have gained an enviable reputation among the lovers of a wholesome and absolutely pure beverage. The most scrupulous cleanliness is observed in all of the different departments, and every care exercised to maintain the high standard of excellence of the product. The latest and most improved machinery is used, and no expense spared to keep in touch with the most progressive methods in the manufacture of beer.

Following the death of Mr. Rochevot, new officers were elected, and if the same popular policy is maintained there is no reason why the present annual output of the brewery will not be materially increased in the near future.

The present officers of the company are: Caroline Rochevot, president; Matilda A. Rochevot, vice-president; Oscar P. Rochevot, secretary.

The J. Schuesler Brewing Co.

O BETTER proof of the phenomenal growth of an industry could be furnished than the increasing business of the John Schuesler Brewing Company since the new management became effective in 1888. Under its progressive policy the volume of business has more than trebled, and is now on a most substantial basis. The brewery has a frontage of 373 feet on Emslie Street, 275 feet on Clinton Street, 51 feet on Eagle Street, and 425 feet on Railroad Avenue. It is equipped with machinery of the most recent and best types known in successful brewing practice. There is one De la Vergne refrigerating machine of 75 tons capacity, as well as a 65-ton Case machine. The necessary driving force is furnished by a Tift engine of 70 horse-power. All of the malting is done on the premises, and the capacity of the malt house alone exceeds 80,000 bushels per year. The buildings are conveniently and compactly situated, so that the handling of the raw material is effected with the minimum amount of labor and cost.

William Simon, the present proprietor, was born in Germany in 1853. His father was a brewer, and it was from him that he gained a valuable insight into the brewing business. In 1871, Mr. Simon arrived in America, where he soon found employment with the well-known brewers, John Schneider, Otto Huber, and Obermeyer & Liebman, of Williamsburg, N. Y. From Williamsburg he went to East Boston, Mass., where he was for some time the valued foreman of Conrad Decker's brewery. His next engagements were with Gerhard Lang, George Rochevot and George Roos, of this city. In 1880, he renewed his connection with Mr. Lang, with whom he remained until May 23, 1888. After a sojourn of three months in the Fatherland, on account of ill-health, Mr. Simon returned to Buffalo to become a partner in the John Schuesler Brewing Company, since which time its prosperity is sufficient evidence of Mr. Simon's business ability and wonderful skill as an expert and scientific brewer. It is safe to say that no brewer in Buffalo works harder or is more conscientious in his efforts to please his customers. How well he is succeeding is best attested by the yearly increase of the business. Mr. Simon has great personal magnetism, and an exceptionally pleasing presence.

The trade for the output of this favorite brewery is largely in Buffalo and contiguous territory, and is energetically looked after by Mr. Simon, who devotes his entire time to the business. Mr. Simon's able and efficient assistant is Joseph G. Schaff, his son-in-law, who is one of Buffalo's bright young business men. Mr. Schaff became connected with the company in 1891, and no inconsiderable share of its prosperity is due to his keen foresight and great executive ability.

The Star Brewery.

The Star Brewery.

SITUATED almost geographically in the center of Buffalo, the Star Brewery is exceptionally favored in location. It has a frontage of 200 feet on Cherry Street, and 150 feet on Spring Street. This is the site of the old Haas Brewery, established in 1860; later known as the Queen City Brewery. Early in 1892 the present firm was established, and the plant named the "Star Brewery." At that time the annual output was 4,000 barrels, which has since increased to 20,000 barrels. Two brands of beer are manufactured, known as "Columbia," and "Standard Lager." They find a ready sale principally in Buffalo, and are especially popular in restaurants, clubs and residences.

The most gratifying feature of the business is the bottling department which the present firm created and rapidly built up to proportions that now compare very favorably with any bottling trade in town. The company has entire control of this branch of the business, which insures the greatest care and cleanliness in putting up the beer. All beers bottled are especially brewed for the purpose. They have an exceedingly fine flavor and are neatly and conveniently put up for table use. The whole equipment of this department is first class in every particular, while the quality of the beer produced more than meets the requirements of the most exacting patrons.

Many improvements have been made in the plant since 1892, and still greater improvements are under consideration. The members of the firm are John L. Schwartz, John S. Kellner, Edward A. Diebolt and Joseph Phillips.

Mr. Schwartz, who is at the head of the business, was born in 1859. Since 1882 he has been a successful business man, and there is no reason to doubt the fulfillment of a most promising future in his chosen career.

Mr. John S. Kellner was born in Dunkirk in 1865, and is a man of varied business experience. He has been uniformly successful in all of his enterprises.

Mr. Edward A. Diebolt was born in Buffalo in 1857, and devotes all of his time to the business. He is industrious and very popular.

Mr. Joseph Phillips was born in Buffalo in 1860, and had had much valuable experience in the office department of the brewing industry before becoming a member of this firm. His work has been eminently satisfactory to his colleagues.

The Christian Weyand Brewing Company.

IN 1866. Christian Weyand established the business now conducted by The Christian Weyand Brewing Company. Mr. Weyand is a native of France, having been born in the province of Lorraine a little more than seventy years ago. There he spent his youth and received his education; but in his twenty-first year he left Lorraine for the wider opportunities of the New World, landing in New York just fifty years ago. He soon found his way to Buffalo, but it was nearly twenty years before he began the business with which his name is now so intimately connected in the minds of all Buffalonians. During these years he worked as a shoemaker—at first as an employee, and later in a shop of his own.

Mr. Weyand, with a partner, began the brewing business in a small way, with little capital and a poorly equipped plant; but the purest and best of barley malt was used from the start, and improved machinery was introduced as fast as the necessary capital could be secured. In 1873, Mr. Weyand assumed entire charge of the business, and applied himself vigorously to the task of building up a model brewery. His efforts met with entire success, and in a few years his establishment became one of the first in its line in Buffalo—a city that boasts of many fine breweries. In 1890 he organized the business into a stock company, called The Christian Weyand Brewing Company, of which he is president, his son, John A. Weyand, vice-president and manager, and another son, Charles M. Weyand, secretary and treasurer. Since then the business has materially increased, and in 1896-97 it became necessary to make extensive additions to the plant. The new buildings on the corner of Main and Goodell streets, built of buff terra cotta elaborately ornamented in Renaissance style, are exceedingly handsome; and it is now one of the best equipped breweries in the country.

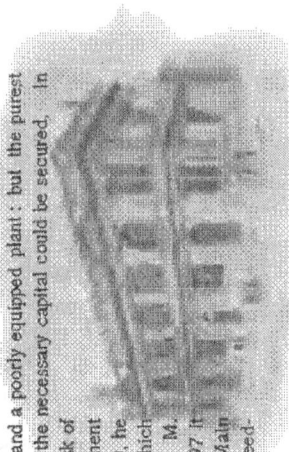

GRAIN ELEVATOR

MALT HOUSE

STORAGE

REFRIGERATED

OFFICE

NE OF THE largest of Buffalo's breweries, in point of capital invested and the volume of business transacted each year, is that of the Phœnix Brewery, owned and operated by the Ziegele Brewing Company. This brewery was established in 1857 by A. Ziegele. Later, Mr. Ziegele's sons assumed control, from whom it was purchased by the present company in 1887.

In 1887, after the organization of the company, a fire devastated their plant in the rear of Main and Virginia streets. Hardly had the damage thus sustained been repaired, when the fire fiend entirely destroyed the balance of the property east of Washington. These calamities only served to spur on to greater endeavors, and necessary steps were at once taken for the erection of absolutely fire-proof buildings, in which was installed a plant, the machinery of which represented all of the modern advances made in the best brewing practice.

The site of the new buildings, which was very properly designated "Phœnix Brewery," is the entire block bounded by Virginia, Washington, Burton and Rochevot streets, having a frontage of over 242 feet on Washington and a depth of 126 feet. The office is situated on the corner of Washington and Virginia streets, and is an artistic two-story structure, commanding a full view of the shipping and receiving departments located in the rear. Next to the office, with a frontage of 80 feet, is the refrigerated storage building, where beer is fermented and aged. The aggregate capacity of the numerous vats and casks enables the company to place only thoroughly fermented and aged beer on the market. Adjoining the refrigerated storage is the brew house, which has a frontage of 40 feet and a height of 90 feet above the curb. In rear of the brew house is located the milling department, fitted with the necessary equipment for the reception and reduction of the grain used in brewing. The operation of brewing is performed in successive stages in the brew house, the top floor having the hot-water tubs, meal hoppers and cooling apparatus, while beneath are the mash tub, copper kettle, etc. The first floor holds the hop jack, pumps, engines, and two large, complicated De la Vergne refrigerating machines. On the opposite side is the boiler house, fitted with three 100 horse-power boilers. The bottling department occupies a building, 40 by 25 feet, on Burton Alley. Over 20 barrels of the famous "Lager" and "Bohemie" brands are bottled daily. The best clubs and residences in Buffalo and adjacent towns consume this output. There is a storage elevator of 50,000 bushels capacity. This group of imposing buildings extends from Virginia Street to Burton Alley, representing an expenditure of over $250,000. The officers are: Geo. A. Lewis, president; Albert Ziegele, Jr., treasurer; Jacob Ditcher, secretary, and Wm. F. Duckwitz, its popular and able manager.

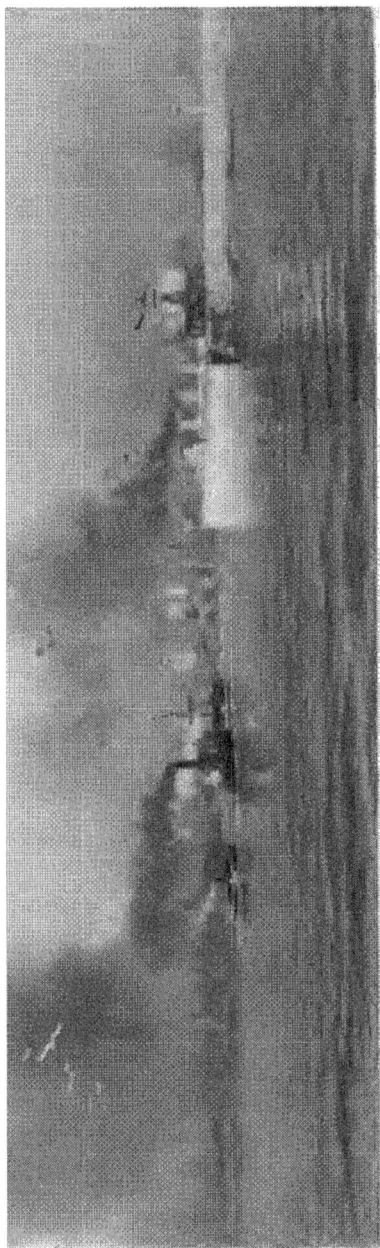

MARINE VIEW OF GREATER BUFFALO.

HE CASUAL visitor to any large American city is usually very little concerned about the details of its early histories, and can hardly be expected to feel any especial interest in the story of its pioneer days. In fact, the history of the origin and primal growth of the Eastern cities of North America, present so many similarities that a person familiar with the record of any one of them can very readily surmise the story of the rise and progress of the others. In one particular, however, the record of Buffalo is unique, and that is its close connection with the events (coupled with its picturesque peculiarities) which make up the history of the Niagara Frontier; and it owes its present importance to the fact that its advantageous location was recognized by a man who looked ahead with the keen foresight of commercial enterprise, rather than with the poetical vision of a romantic day-dreamer. Of Joseph Ellicott, the founder of Buffalo, it has been said, that "his ideas were based upon an almost prophetic perception of the future growth of Western New York." It thus might well be added, "as a practical man with practical thoughts, he saw the tide of progress flowing westward, and discerned the possibilities of Buffalo as a Nature-favored site for the chosen gateway through which that tide must flow."

In its earliest village days, Buffalo was known as New Amster-dam; a name given it by the Holland Land Company, which controlled so much territory in New York State a century ago, but by act of legisla-ture March 11, 1808, Buffalo became the legal name of the county seat of Niagara County, which was then created.

During the closing days of the year 1813, Buffalo was burned by the British. After the British had been finally disposed of, a new start was made and Buffalo had a small boom. The Erie Canal route was surveyed and Buffalo was chosen as the western terminus. Buffalo had

ERIE COUNTY BANK BUILDING.

MASONIC TEMPLE.

MOONEY-BRISBANE BUILDING.

been incorporated as a village April 2, 1813, re-organized in 1815, and again in 1822. The Erie Canal was completed October 24, 1825, but has since been greatly improved, a vast amount of money having been expended by the State for that purpose. Two years ago an appropriation of $9,000,000 was made for deepening the channel and lengthening the locks, which work is now well under way.

April 20, 1832, Buffalo having at that time more than 10,000 inhabitants, was incorporated as a city. A natural question for a visitor to ask is, "Where did Buffalo get its name?" or "Why was the place called Buffalo?" Learned men have discussed this question long and earnestly, but without arriving at any positive solution of the problem, but it appears to be generally conceded by all who have given the matter any serious consideration, that the selection of the name had some sort of connection with the existence in these parts at some time in the dim and fading past of the American buffalo, the *Bison Americanus*. The writer suggests that it is not impossible that the name came down from the French pioneers of the days of La Salle and Hennepin, as the French words *"Boeuf-el-l'eau"* sound in the vernacular exceedingly like "Buff-a-lo." The matter is not one of particular significance, as Buffalo, by any other name, would have grown as great as she now is, with a promise of still further greatness.

The growth of Buffalo for nearly half a century after attaining its cityhood was comparatively slow, but when its former Mayor, Grover Cleveland, entered the White House for his first Presidential term, March 4, 1885, Buffalo was then described "a kind of half-way house between the East and West. It was a city of 160,000 inhabitants, with a considerable trade and having valuable commercial facilities for some of the big railroads of the State, and for the lake shipping gathered at that point. It had two places of amusement, eight daily newspapers, four of them in German, a seating room founded in 1862, several hotels and a number of commemorative monuments."

But, since 1885, the growth of Buffalo has been phenomenal, even compared with the growth of other great industrial centers. Its population during the last twelve years has increased 52 per cent. In the same period New York increased only 25, St. Louis 29, Philadelphia 23, and

PARADE GROUNDS.

MORGAN BUILDING.

THE FRONT.

Cincinnati 16. In the number of manufacturing establishments during this period, Buffalo is said to have increased 200 per cent., the figures for the other cities of the country being New York 124 per cent., Chicago 183, Boston 116, Philadelphia 112, Cincinnati 134, Brooklyn 103, St. Louis 110, and Baltimore 43.

The United States census of 1890 gave Buffalo a population of 278,796. In May, 1895, a very carefully taken police census gave 335,705 as the figures. A very conservative estimate places the growth during 1895, 1896 and up to date at 30,000, so that the present population may be fairly claimed to be not less than 365,000.

In the number of people employed in manufactories, Buffalo has increased 178 per cent. New York 55, Boston 53, Philadelphia 36. Baltimore 47. In the value of its manufactured products Buffalo has increased 124 per cent., and in the wages paid to those engaged in manufactures 226 per cent., Cincinnati 126, Baltimore 133, New York 136, Boston 124 and Brooklyn 175. In respect to the material used in manufactures, Buffalo has increased 86 per cent. in twelve years. New York increasing 24, Philadelphia 52, Brooklyn 7, Baltimore 53, Boston 28 and Cincinnati 33.

These surprising increases do not, however, exhaust the list of what Buffalo has gained since Cleveland left it in 1885. Buffalo claims to have more asphalt pavement than any other city in the world, more miles of railroad trackage within its limits than any other city, the cheapest water power in the world, 900 acres of park system, 147 miles of street railroad system. 125 miles of stone and 153 miles of concrete pavement, besides cheap coal, natural gas, a low tax-rate, 21 steam railroads and a present population of 365,000, the figures growing rapidly all the time. In one respect, at least, however, Buffalo has fallen off since Cleveland left it, the mortality rate being only seventeen per thousand, much lower than any other city.

As has already been intimated, this remarkable growth has been due to Buffalo's geographical position at the eastern terminus of the great lakes, by virtue of which she has become the gateway, both by land and water, of the vast traffic arising from the development of the

DELAWARE AVENUE.

FIREMEN'S MONUMENT.

DELAWARE AVENUE.

enormous resources of the West and Northwest. The East required the lumber, wheat, corn and other grains, the cattle and sheep, the ores and metals and other products of the West and Northwest, while they, in turn, enforced a reciprocal demand for coal, manufactured metals and textiles, and merchandise of all kinds.

The first vessel to sail the lakes was the sixty-ton craft built by the explorer La Salle, on Cayuga Creek, near Niagara Falls. He called it the "Griffon," and sailed her up the Niagara River and out on Lake Erie, August 17, 1679. Other vessels of small tonnage sailed the lakes eighty years ago, but the marine traffic in and out of Buffalo was comparatively insignificant until the advent of the "steam era." The first lake steamer, the "Walk-in-the-Water," a crude affair, was launched at Black Rock, May 28, 1818, and did some service for two seasons thereafter, but was wrecked off the Buffalo lighthouse, November 1, 1821.

Since 1821 many thousand vessels have sailed into and out of Buffalo harbor. The tonnage of the port of Buffalo, December 31, 1896, as shown by the Custom House records, was 191,128.83 tons. 385 vessels, of which 257 are steamers.

To accommodate the growing vessel traffic of Buffalo continuous and costly improvements in the harbor and on the breakwater have been necessary. The total amount expended by the United States for these purposes up to June 30, 1896, was $2,703,507.93, and a further expenditure of $2,200,000 has been authorized for work now in progress. Major Thomas W. Symons, the U. S. Engineer in charge, in an official report made in September, 1896, said: "The commerce of Buffalo, which is enormous, depends entirely upon the work of harbor improvement done by the United States. During the year the departures and arrivals of vessels by lake and river aggregated in number 9,975, and in tonnage 9,612,423 tons." Some idea of what the new harbor will mean to the Buffalo of the future may be gathered from the statement that when the breakwater is finally completed, there will be capacity behind it for 50

STATE HOSPITAL

GUARANTY BUILDING.

MASTEN PARK HIGH SCHOOL.

new docks, each with a frontage of 200 feet and a length of 1,000 feet, with 200 foot slips between. This will give a total wharfage capacity in the outer harbor of 110,000 linear feet, or nearly 21 miles. The inner harbor, consisting principally of the Buffalo River, with wharfage of about five miles, the City Ship Canal, with four miles, and the Tifft Farm property, with two miles, adds eleven miles more of wharfage, and with the other dockage in Erie Basin and along the river the total wharfage capacity of Buffalo Harbor five years hence will be over 40 miles. And the wharfage in the outer harbor will be the best on the lakes.

The importance to Buffalo of the Erie Canal may be estimated when it is stated that in 1896 1,172,552 tons of merchandise, valued at $31,608,123, were carried between Buffalo and New York.

Its waterways, important as they are, by no means comprise all of Buffalo's traffic advantages. It is one of the greatest railroad centers of the United States. The yards of its 27 roads cover 3,600 acres within the city alone and represent a capital invested of over $100,000,000.

Here are some cold facts about Buffalo lake, canal and rail commerce :

Due to its railroads, Buffalo has become the second largest live-stock market in the world. It leads as a sheep market and is second as a cattle and a hog market. The receipts for 1896 were: of sheep 2,664,200 head, a gain in ten years of about 43 per cent., and of cattle 945,274 head, a gain in ten years of nearly 100 per cent., and an increase over 1895 of 149,424 head. Buffalo is also one of the largest markets in the world for horses.

Buffalo is the largest coal-distributing market in the world. In 1896 the coal receipts were over 7,275,901 tons and the exports over 2,402,128 tons. Over $10,000,000 have been invested in terminal facilities for coal, which have a total shipping capacity of 27,500 tons a day.

Buffalo is the second largest grain market in the world. The receipts last year were 214,937,553 bushels, a gain over 1895 of 32 per cent. In 1896 15,000,000 more bushels were sent east on the Erie Canal alone than in 1895. Buffalo's 52 grain

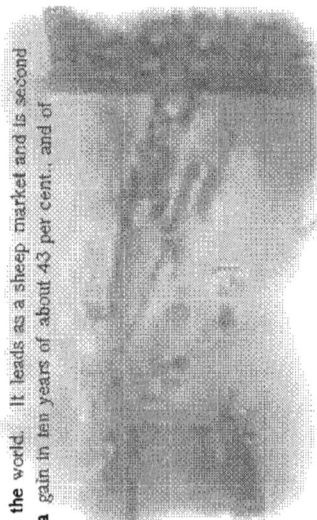

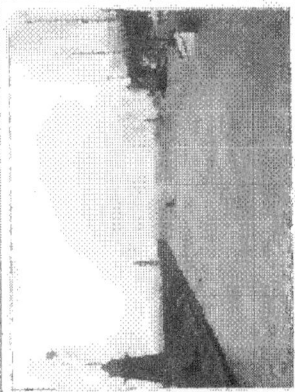

BUFFALO HARBOR.

SOLDIERS' MONUMENT.

BUFFALO HARBOR.

elevators have a combined storage capacity of 16,550,000 bushels, which will be increased to over 20,000,000 bushels by the close of the summer. Two million bushels of grain have been unloaded and the vessels again loaded with coal, in 24 hours, at our docks.

Buffalo is the largest market for flour in the world, and it is sure to become the largest milling city on the continent. Flouring mills have increased and multiplied in recent years at a tremendous rate.

Besides all this. Buffalo is fast assuming great importance as a manufacturing center, which is a natural outcome of her shipping facilities, and her proximity to a great variety of raw material. Some of the leading manufactures are car wheels, bicycles, marine boilers and engines, lake steamers, agricultural implements, flour, wall paper, iron bridges, malt, cast-iron pipe, refrigerators, soap, starch, medicines, leather, illuminating oils, scales, stoves, etc., and not the least noteworthy of her business enterprises are her numerous complete and extensive brewing plants, a more extended mention of which is made elsewhere.

Buffalo people are naturally proud of their city, and give five great reasons why it is the best city in the world to live in.

FIRST.—It is the most healthful city. Buffalo's health record is regarded by the medical world as phenomenal, and it has given the city a world-wide reputation. In 1896 the death rate reached 12.72, which is the lowest of any city of any size on the continent. Buffalo's health department is the most efficient to be found anywhere.

SECOND.—It is the most beautiful city. Buffalo is one of the handsomest residence cities in the world. Its streets are wide and beautifully shaded, and it is noted everywhere for its many miles of smoothly paved asphalt streets and avenues, containing more miles than Paris, London, Washington or any other city in the world. The Buffalo Park system embraces over a thousand acres and more than 17 miles of beautiful park driveway. Delaware Avenue is one of the famous streets in the world.

THIRD.—It is the coolest city in summer. During the torrid season last summer, when, in every other city in the country, people were dying by the score from the awful heat. Buffalo was

COAL DOCK.

BUILDERS' EXCHANGE.

LUMBER DOCK.

enjoying the cool breezes of Lake Erie and its citizens going about their daily business in comparative ease and comfort. Only one death occurred during that period that could in any way be laid to the account of the heat.

The fourth reason is best shown by a glance at the map of North America with reference to the position of Buffalo upon it, at the same time remembering that many millions of dollars are being expended at the present time in improving Buffalo Harbor and the Erie Canal, so as to put both in readiness to handle a traffic in grain, coal, lumber, and ores to which the past immense volume of trade will in a few years seem trivial in comparison.

Lastly, it is the best city in the world to live in, because, in the words of Nicolas Tesla. " Niagara power will make Buffalo the greatest city in the world!"

But everybody cannot make Buffalo their home. There are a good many people who think their home city, if not the best in the world, is at least as good as Buffalo and better than a good many others. So, let us put an end to booming Buffalo and give the visitor-reader hereof some idea of what to see and how to see it while he or she is making a brief stay in the Queen City of the Lakes.

To those who like to see how grain is handled, an hour or two spent upon the docks watching the great elevators loading and unloading wheat and corn will not be an unpleasing experience. If you are interested in cattle, sheep or horses, the live stock market at East Buffalo is well worth visiting. If you are curious about big buildings, or are on the lookout for architectural pointers, it will not be without interest if you look around the City and County Building, the D. S. Morgan Building, the Guaranty Building, the Erie County Savings Bank, the Board of Trade Building, the Hotel Iroquois, the Library Building, Real Estate Exchange, Builders' Exchange, the Mooney and Brisbane Building, the Grosvenor Library and the Ellicott Square Building. These are some of the most notable of the more modern structures in Buffalo. There are, besides, many fine churches, schools and hospitals, but in these the casual visitor is not usually especially interested. At the Library Building, in addition to

commodious reading rooms and a reference library open to the public, will be found an interesting historical collection, and an excellent display made by the Natural Sciences Society. The library and gymnasium of the German Young Men's Society in Music Hall are worthy of a visit. The Ellicott Square block is said to be the largest office building in the world.

A fine view of the city, river and harbor is to be had from the roof of some of the tallest of the buildings mentioned.

If you ride a wheel, you will declare you have found Buffalo a wheelman's Paradise, or if you prefer a carriage ride, there are over two hundred miles of beautiful streets paved with asphalt and lined with shade trees, with pleasant and many elegant homes on either side, and, better still, is the splendid park system of 950 acres, extending from the City and County Building northward to the Front and the U. S. military headquarters at Fort Porter, thence eastward to the Buffalo Park and further eastward, along the broad parkways, to the Parade. South-east of the city is another park system that is being rapidly beautified.

The city covers an area of 42 square miles, and after leaving the business section, on the west, the north, the northeast and some portions of the southeast, the visitor will encounter nothing but well-paved and pleasant thoroughfares.

The street-car service will be found to be a generally good one, the electric trolley system only being used, the fare being only five cents a trip, with a free transfer system. On the Belt Line steam railroad system of the New York Central Company which runs around the city, the uniform rate of five cents for the trip is also made.

From Buffalo enjoyable excursions can be made out in the harbor; across the river to Fort Erie into Canada, either from Ferry Street or the foot of Main Street; to Crystal Beach on the Canadian shore of Lake Erie; to Woodlawn Beach on the American shore of Lake Erie, and to other pleasure resorts along the lake shore; to Chautauqua Lake, 70 miles southwest; to Silver Lake, about the same distance southeast;

PARADE HOUSE.

PARK LAKE.

to Portage Falls; to the Kinzua Bridge; to various pleasure resorts and fishing grounds along the Niagara River, including points on Grand Island; to Fort Niagara, to Toronto, and, last and best of all, to Niagara Falls, of which more is said in another place.

But all these matters do not make up the sum total of Buffalo's advantages and attractions, and the future visitor will find that the advantages are being developed and the attractions enhanced very rapidly. Several exceptionally fine buildings are in the early stages of construction, the most important of which are the new Government building, which will cost $2,000,000, a new Armory for the 74th Regiment, National Guard, which will cost $400,000, and which, it is claimed, will be the largest and finest armory in the world, a new building for the Historical Society, several new mammoth grain elevators, and a half a dozen steam and electric railway extensions. Several million dollars is also being spent in doing away with the railroad crossings at grade within the city limits; the Union railway depot is being re-constructed and enlarged, and many other public enterprises involving vast expenditures of money and great labor are contemplated or have actually been decided upon. Buffalo, therefore, is not likely to stand still, for many years to come at least.

CLINTON MARKET.

REAL ESTATE EXCHANGE.

CHIPPEWA MARKET.

Up-to-Date Facts about Buffalo.

Buffalo is the second city of the Empire State.

Is a great convention city.

Has a handsome City and County Hall which cost $4,500,000.

Will soon have a new Post-Office.

Has several beautiful cemeteries and a crematory.

Area of city — 42 square miles,

Population, over 365,000.

Has 9 theatres, many public halls, 60 public schools, 180 churches

Has 48 hotels and 5 public markets.

Has 15 hospitals and infirmaries, and many asylums.

Has an inexhaustible pure water supply. Waterworks property valued at over $7,000,000.

Has possession of unlimited electric power; part of which is generated at Niagara Falls.

Has about 3,500 manufactories, and 100,000 operatives.

Has 930 acres of park and 17 miles of park driveways.

Has 100 miles, perfect system, of electric street railways.

Has 700 miles railway track, 27 lines.

Has 230 miles of asphalted streets, besides 125 miles of stone and brick.

Has two State armories; another now in course of construction of mammoth proportions.

Has several commercial organizations.

Local Weather Bureau is the finest equipped in the United States.

Has trolley lines to Niagara Falls, Williamsville, Pine Hill, Lancaster, Depew, Gardenville, West Seneca, Blaisdell and other suburbs.

Streets lighted with gas and electricity.

Has very cheap coal and natural gas in abundance.

Is the most healthful large city in the United States; death rate for 1896, 12.72 per 1,000.

Has 52 elevators, etc.; storage capacity, 16,690,000 bushels.

Has 12 flour mills; capacity, 8,000 barrels daily; barrels manufactured, 1896, 1,224,699.

Has the largest coal trestle in the world, nearly one mile long.

Has five iron ore docks, besides many coal docks and coal pockets.

Has 18 commercial banks; capital, $4,850,000; surplus, $4,076,170,00.

Has four savings banks; assets, $40,146,972.58.

Has two trust companies; capital, $700,000; deposits, $5,534,351.00.

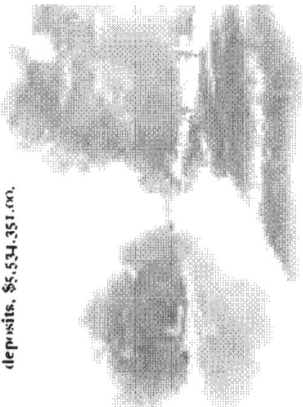

BUFFALO HARBOR.

LAFAYETTE AVENUE PRESBYTERIAN CHURCH.

BUFFALO HARBOR.

Up-to-Date Facts about Buffalo Continued

Bank Clearings, $219,491,646,60; balances, $38,653,847.71.

Has two free and several other libraries, a Fine Arts Academy, many colleges and clubs, a Historical Society, a Masonic Temple, and a Society of Natural Sciences.

Exports by lake, 1896, 2,490,068 tons coal, 670,713 barrels cement and plaster, 621,287 barrels salt, and 1,204,887 barrels sugar.

Coal receipts, 1896, 7,274,991 tons.

Customs' receipts, 1896, $368,770.77.

Post-office receipts, 1896, $708,955.78.

Lumber receipts, 1896, 610,372,884 feet.

Live Stock receipts, 1896, 7,600,224 head; largest cattle market in the world.

Internal Revenue receipts, 1896, $1,084,040,93.

Grain and Flax Seed receipts, 1896, by lake, 172,474,664 bushels.

Flour — largest depot in the world — receipts by lake in 1896, 10,384,184 barrels and packages.

Vessels arrived in 1896, 5,581; tonnage, 5,634,494; vessels cleared in 1896, 5,741; tonnage, 5,670,248. Total vessels, 11,322; total tonnage, 11,304,742.

Tonnage of the port, 1896, 385 vessels, of 191,128.83 tonnage.

In 1896, a steamer brought to this port a cargo of 206,673 bushels of corn; and another 176,803 bushels of wheat — largest cargoes ever known.

Elevators in 1896 handled 170,963,131 bushels of grain and flaxseed.

Length of breakwater, 7,608 feet at present; to be extended to Stony Point.

Rate of taxation in 1897 — City, $14.18 on valuation of $1,000. Real estate and personal property, $247,388,275.00.

CANAL BOATS.

MERCHANTS' EXCHANGE.

COAL TRESTLE.

NIAGARA FALLS.

AMERICAN FALLS.   NIAGARA FALLS.   HORSESHOE FALLS.

FACTS ABOUT NIAGARA FALLS.

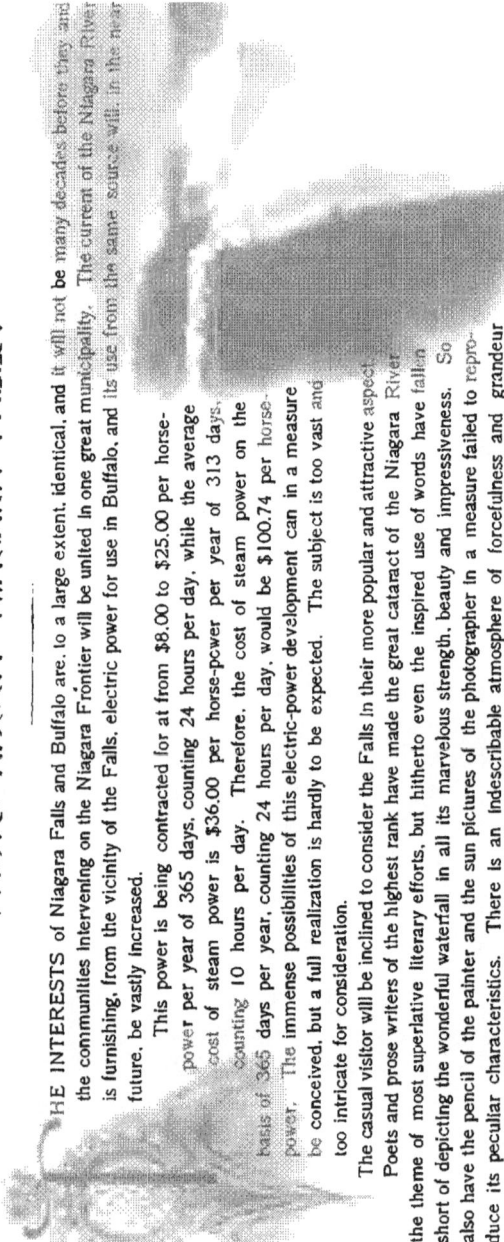

HE INTERESTS of Niagara Falls and Buffalo are. to a large extent. identical, and it will not be many decades before they and the communities intervening on the Niagara Frontier will be united in one great municipality. The current of the Niagara River is furnishing, from the vicinity of the Falls, electric power for use in Buffalo, and its use from the same source will in the near future, be vastly increased.

This power is being contracted for at from $8.00 to $25.00 per horse-power per year of 365 days, counting 24 hours per day, while the average cost of steam power is $36.00 per horse-power per year of 313 days, counting 10 hours per day. Therefore, the cost of steam power on the basis of 365 days per year, counting 24 hours per day, would be $100.74 per horse-power. The immense possibilities of this electric-power development can in a measure be conceived, but a full realization is hardly to be expected. The subject is too vast and too intricate for consideration.

The casual visitor will be inclined to consider the Falls in their more popular and attractive aspect. Poets and prose writers of the highest rank have made the great cataract of the Niagara River the theme of most superlative literary efforts, but hitherto even the inspired use of words have fallen short of depicting the wonderful waterfall in all its marvelous strength. beauty and impressiveness. So also have the pencil of the painter and the sun pictures of the photographer in a measure failed to reproduce its peculiar characteristics. There is an indescribable atmosphere of forcefulness and grandeur

ALONG THE GORGE.

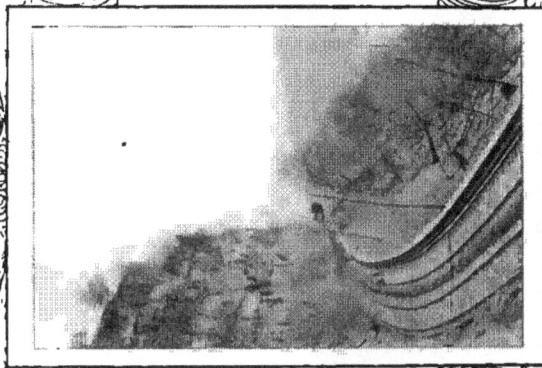

ALONG THE GORGE.

ALONG THE GORGE.

environing the huge mass of rushing, tumbling waters which cannot be depicted in verse, in prose or in pictures. In the blunt but emphatic language of the showman, "The Falls must be seen and seen again to be appreciated."

But while the waters come pouring down the river from the great lakes and sweeping over the falls, as they have done for ages, in recent years there have been vast changes in the surroundings. The artifices of man have been and are still being combined with the forces of Nature in adding to and modulating the beauties of the place, and bringing order out of the chaos of attractions that have long made the place famous in connection with the huge cataract itself. On both sides of the river parks, under proper supervision, have been laid out. July 15, 1885, the State Reservation on the American side was formally opened for the free use of the public, and May 24, 1888, Queen Victoria Park on the Canadian side was formally opened to the general public.

Besides these two great observation grounds from which the Falls may be viewed in all their varying aspects, there are a number of minor points and places of interest. The chief of these are the new Suspension Bridge connecting Canada with the United States, the Cantilever and railway suspension bridges at Suspension Bridge, and the Whirlpool Rapids and Whirlpool, and the Gorge beyond. There are a number of outside museums and elevators; but the most important of the extra attractions of the Falls is the Observation Tower, opposite Prospect Park, 300 feet high. From the upper platform a view is obtained unequaled in the world for grandeur and picturesque variety.

Another pleasing experience is a trip on one of the two Maids of the Mist. Niagara Falls itself has been greatly improved in recent years. It is no longer a sleepy country village, but is justly putting on metropolitan airs, having recently been organized in association with Suspension Bridge as a city, with all a modern city's duties, privileges and progressive spirit. The most important factor in attaining this municipal result has been the construction of the great hydraulic tunnel for the purpose of utilizing the enormous and continuous water force of Niagara River to supply power for manufacturing and other purposes, with the electric current as the grand medium. The principle upon which the tunnel has been

built is exceedingly simple. The tunnel, which is subterranean, is really a great tail race extending about a mile, from the water level at a point of Niagara River above the Falls, and embouching below the Falls at a much lower level. The tunnel is connected with the river by short surface canals, wheel pits and cross tunnels, the pits being furnished with turbines and the necessary hydraulic machinery, dynamos, etc., for generating and transmitting the electric power-giving current.

Buffalo and Niagara Falls are only 22 miles apart. Travel between the two points is rapid and convenient, either by boat on the picturesque Niagara River, by the steam cars of the New York Central, the Michigan Central, the West Shore, the Erie and the Lehigh Valley railroads, or by the electric trolley line which is an adjunct of the street railway system of Buffalo, connecting with the Niagara Falls and Suspension Bridge system, and also with the Gorge Route of the Niagara Falls and Lewiston line.

It will, no doubt, be interesting to those who receive this Souvenir to know that it is proposed to hold a Pan-American Exposition, to illustrate, on a large scale, the progress that has been made in the New World during the nineteenth century, at some suitable point on the Niagara Frontier. The site most favored is Cayuga Island, a very beautiful place, with excellent advantages, located a short distance south of Niagara Falls. The Exposition will be opened from May until October, 1899; and the enterprise is being carried out by a number of leading capitalists of New York, Buffalo and Niagara Falls.

R. C. HILL.

www.ingramcontent.com/pod-product-compliance
Lightning Source LLC
Chambersburg PA
CBHW020333090426
42735CB00009B/1525